NUKED BY NARCISSIST

WHEN THE MASK FINALLY FALLS

La Morena

La Morena
Nuked by Narcissist

All rights reserved
Copyright © 2024 by **La Morena**

Published by BooxAi
ISBN: 978-965-578-871-6

This book is dedicated to all of my wonderful children and grandchildren who have walked this journey alongside me, adding to my many reasons to strive to be a better person.

Contents

Chapter One

THE COLOR OF gRAY
THE GRANDIOSE NARCISSIST

In a world of teenage dreams and schemes,
A tale of deception and forbidden themes.
He lied about his age to get me, oh what a ploy,
I was only 16, he was 20, oh boy!
Attracted to his Vanilla Ice and Color Me Badd,
And all the other soulful White boys, my head had.
With swagger that made hearts go mad,
His tongue, so slick, in ways untold,
he made my toes curl and legs unfold.
He had a way with words, so smooth and sly,
I fell for his lies, oh my, oh my!
Defying my parents, I took the leap,
Hook, line, and sinker, I fell in deep.
The first time we shared an intimate whirl,
Proved to be too much for a garden-green naive young girl.

Southern Hospitality

I ran away from home, not an abusive one,
But principled, seeking freedom and fun.
Little did I know, my parents had a reason,
To shield me from a world of narcissistic treason.
His family, oh what a sight to behold,
A chain-smoking mother, her stories untold.
Whenever she left a room, you'd see,
The Marlboro man in a cloud of smoke, so free.
A racist from the South, Savannah, Georgia,
Living in a world of cotton-picking euphoria.
Fiery as the lighters she owned,
Her words, like fire, were always thrown.
The father, a devoted mediocre man,
Limited education, but never mistreated me, understand.
And then there was the sibling, oh so charming,
With the swagger of his older narcissistic sibling, quite disarming.
But easier on the eyes, I must confess,
Still, I felt like a puzzle piece, out of place, I guess.

So off I went, seeking my own path,
Unaware of the narcissist's deceptive wrath.
Little did I know, the lies he would tell,
And how he would lead me into a forbidden spell.
But hey, let's not dwell on the gloom,
For this is just the beginning of my humorous zoom.
Stay tuned for more tales of teenage bliss,
And the lessons learned from a narcissist kiss.

Traded Love for Instability

My parents tried everything they could,
But I was smitten, oh what a fool,
For the grandiose narcissist, so cool.
I left each time I could, to be with him,
Ignoring the warnings, life looked so grim.
Religious leaders and police, they tried,
To counsel me, to open my eyes wide.
But I was stubborn, and in love's trance,
I couldn't see the truth; I took a chance.
And then I got pregnant, a baby on the way,
A ticket to freedom, or so I would say.
At seventeen, I thought I'd be emancipated,
I wore my parents down, they were exasperated.
But guilt still lingers, for my father's stroke,
I caused him stress, it's a heavy yoke.
Yet, in my young mind, I felt nothing but glee,
For now, I was free, with the man I loved, you see.
Love bombing had worked, I was under his spell,

I thought I had found heaven, oh well.
Little did I know, the truth would unfold,
In the story yet untold.

The Grandiose Embarrassment

In a world of deceit, the narcissist thrived,
Spinning tales of wealth, where truth was contrived.
He'd flaunt his play money, with a flashy display,
But deep down, I knew it was all just a charade.
His lies were unwarranted, a web he would weave,
Claiming assets we lacked, just to deceive.
Three real dollars, he'd place on top,
With play money beneath, a deceptive prop.
Embarrassment filled my mind, but my lips stayed sealed,
For challenging his falsehoods, I never revealed.

THE MODERN-DAY SLAVE

Little by little, the price of rebellion grew,
As I ignored my parents' advice, it's true.
Verbal and physical abuse came my way,
From the man I loved, who was always astray.
I chose him over school, what a mistake,
Missing out on education, my future at stake.
Working two low-paid jobs, barely any sleep,
On the city bus, exhaustion ran deep.
Where was my knight in shining armor, I wondered,
But he was with another, my heart plundered.
Was I just a naive girl, a modern-day slave?
Missing only the plantation, where he'd misbehave.
Lashings, both emotional and physical, he'd inflict,
A cruel master, my life he'd constrict.
But now I see the humor in this tale,
A comedy of errors, where I'd often fail.

The Unconditional Love

With the arrival of my little one, joy filled the air,
A son, my heart's delight, a love beyond compare.
Estranged from family, a choice not theirs to make,
Shame and pride, a lethal mix, caused the bond to break.
Back to work I went, before my body could heal,
Disrespected and tormented, the pain was all too real.
Intimacy, a distant memory, a mere facade,
No love, no connection, just a charade.
Embarrassed at every job, meetings I would attend,
The narcissist mischief, a never-ending trend.
But through it all, my love for my child remained,
A beacon of hope, a love that never waned.
Amid chaos, I found strength and grace,
And in my little one's eyes, I found a hopeful place.

THE EVIL MOTHER-IN-LAW

But oh, what a twist, what a surprise,
For the narcissist, a monster in disguise!
Morals were tossed out the window, it's true,
As we were sneaking around, underage and askew.
But then, a baby came into the mix,
And suddenly, marriage became a quick fix.
Dark days descended, as the mother-in-law,
Took control of the baby, leaving me in awe.
My chest would leak at work, oh what a sight,
But alas, breastfeeding was banned, what a plight!
The evil mother-in-law, with her twisted mind,
Accuse me, the heroine of being sexually inclined.
She aimed to break the bond, so strong and new,
For she had failed with her own sons, it's sad but true.
Inexperienced and alone, I did dwell,
With no emotional support, in a dark, lonely cell.
Between random blows, love bombing would appear,
And then, a baby girl, bringing both joy and fear.

Stay tuned for the next entry, my friend,
As our story continues, with twists and turns to no end.
You are wondering if I will ever find a way out of this mess?
Or will the monster's grip tighten, causing distress?

No Laughing Matter

In a world of unexpected pranks and jests,
A brother-in-law's joke put me to the test.
He called from his girlfriend's house, oh what a trick,
Pretending to be my sneaky link, oh so slick.
I returned from work, unaware of the plot,
But my mother-in-law couldn't wait, oh what a shot.
Accusing me of having a secret beau,
Down the hallway I walked, feeling quite low.
And then, in my bedroom, a surprise awaited,
A clothesline moves, like W.W.E, I was fated.
My screams filled the air, my pain so real,
But my mother-in-law egged it on with zeal.
I cried the whole day, my heart filled with sorrow,
And when my brother-in-law returned, no apology to
borrow.
His explanation fell flat, no consolation in sight,
Oh, what a prank, what a terrible night.
But fear not, dear reader, for this is just the start,

In the world of gRay, where humor plays its part.
Stay tuned for more laughs, more twists and turns,
As we delve into the life of a narcissist, oh how it churns.

THE SHADY ROBBERY

Oh, what a tale of woe and trickery,
When the narcissist's lies were plain to see.
He claimed he was robbed, his wallet gone,
But his deceitful ways were soon to be known.
With a performance so grand, he played his part,
But the truth was revealed, a stolen heart.
For he had been with a lady of the night,
And she took his belongings, oh what a sight!
No bruises or marks, just a face rubbed raw,
His fake story crumbling, his act a flaw.
And amidst the abuse and curable STDS,
The mask of deception began to cease.
Fed up and weary, a plan did unfold,
To rid oneself of these menaces who were considered bold.
But fear not, dear reader, for humor shall prevail,
In this tale of deceit, we'll find our tale's trail.

THE TROUBLESOME
REVELATION

Oh, what a twist of fate, so divine,
When a diary's secrets were no longer mine.
My mother-in-law, oh what a sight,
She stumbled upon my plans one night.
She read my words, filled with disdain,
For her son, a narcissist, causing me pain.
She called my parents, scared and afraid,
Begging them to rescue me from this charade.
But alas, my parents played a trick,
They said, "Tag, you're it!" Oh, what a kick!
Perhaps they thought of my past rebellious ways,
And decided to leave me in this maze.
But fear not, for my plan was not in vain,
For my son, locked away, would remain.
In my mother-in-law's room, night after night,
A deadly plan foiled, but still a humorous sight.
Oh, the irony of it all, so grand,
A divine intervention, not as I planned.

But through it all, I find some glee,
In this comedy of errors, for all to see.

THE APRON STRINGS WERE CUT

In a twist of fate, my mother-in-law's brush with death,
Led to her urging her narcissistic son to leave her nest.
Finally, we were free from her controlling grip,
But little did I know, my troubles were about to flip.
At first, the peace was bliss, I didn't mind his lack of work,
But soon I realized, he was more of a pimp than a jerk.
He urged me to work in a strip club, for more money to
make,
But I was blind to the fact, it was all for his own sake.
Brainwashed, gaslighted and fearful, I didn't see the truth,
There was no "us," just me, living in a twisted booth.
My morals were shattered, my strength was broken,
This man and his family had left me heartbroken.
Looking back now, I see the signs were clear,
I was seeking an escape, a way out of this fear.
Like the underground railroad, I longed for freedom's call,
To break free from this mess, this marriage was my downfall.

The Unwanted Guests

Oh, what a bombshell of a night,
When two women came, causing a fright.
One older, with a gun in hand,
Searching for her daughter, oh so grand.
The other, young and full of facts,
About the affair, that's what she cracks.
The narcissist's mask was hanging loose,
His true colors shining through, no excuse.
I planned my escape, I had enough,
No more love, just loathing, yeah tough.

THE GRANDIOSE FINALE

I left, making sure he felt the shame,
Humiliated, his ego was in flames.
Before he passed in 2022,
He admitted his mistreatment, it's true.
But apology or not, it's all in the past,
For he died alone, his body unclaimed, aghast.
Aging poorly, his looks all gone,
A fitting end for a narcissist, so long!

CHAPTER TWO

Cop Out
Covert Narcissist

Oh, what a beautiful sight,
When a cop walked in, shining so bright.
Tall and handsome, with a uniform so neat,
He made my heart skip a beat.
His presence made me feel safe and secure,
And his smile, oh so pure.
We talked for hours, sharing our stories,
Creating memories, full of glories.
He bought only a coffee, just two dollars,
And left a tip, five dollars, for him it was no bother.
I appreciated his generosity,
As a single mom, it brought me glee.
No lazy narcissist in my life,
Just roommates and fun, no more strife.
I was healing and having a blast,
No physical encounters, unless I asked.
But this cop, oh, he was something special,
With his authoritative figure, so influential.
He made me laugh, he made me smile,

And I knew this could be worthwhile.
So, let's see where this story goes,
As the cop and I continue to grow.
In this chapter of love and laughter,
We'll see what happens. Is there a possible happily ever after?

A Love Bombing Fiasco

Oh, what a whirlwind romance,
With a cop so charming and entrancing,
No flaws in sight, he seemed so grand,
But little did I know, it was all a plan.
Love bombing, oh so real,
He swept me off my feet, I couldn't deal,
Promising to rescue me from my wild ways,
But little did I know, it was just a phase.
Irresponsible and foolish, I had been,
Pregnant with another's child, a sin,
Yet this cop still wanted me, it seemed,
But was it love or just a dream?
He vowed to help me grow up fast,
To leave behind my playful past,
But rebellion still lingered in my soul,
And an illegitimate child took its toll.
In my heart, I believed his desire,
But was it true or was he just a liar?

Oh, the cop-out, what a twist,
In this love bombing fiasco, I was blissfully missed.

Too Good to Be True

Oh, what a graduation day,
With a cop by my side,
He cheered me on, encouraged me,
To reach for the stars, to never hide.
Proudly, I walked across that stage,
A big and pregnant college graduate,
With photos to capture the joy,
Of a new chapter, a promising fate.
After my third child was born,
Showered with gifts, love so true,
An instant dad, changing diapers,
In the middle of the night, he'd be there too.
A stepdad also to my other two.
Helping me obtain what I desired,
A driver's license, GED, and college diploma,
Things my first husband had conspired.
For so long, love from another man,
Seemed so wrong, against the norm,

But then I met this cop, so special,
And my heart began to transform.

A Comedy of Errors

Oh, what a comedy it became,
With a cop who couldn't commit,
Years went by, no problems in sight,
Two more babies, one tragic loss.
But still, I hoped for a ring,
Marriage talk, always from me,
But no commitment, just inconsistency.
I proudly claimed to be his fiancé,
But someone said, after 7 years, it's not true,
Inconsistencies grew, devaluing began,
Complaints about family, complaints about work,
Just complaints, complaints, complaints.
Then one day, a text on his beeper,
He leapt across the room, suspicion arose,
"Oh no, not again!" I thought,
The cop who couldn't stay true,
A comedy of errors, that's what it became,
With a cop who seemingly found a way to cop out.

A Beeping Betrayal

Oh, what a twist of fate,
With a beeper that sealed his fate,
I discovered his secret, oh what a blow,
Harriett, the name that I now know.
I could hear her smirk on the other end of the line,
What lies had she been fed, that were oh so fine?
Did she see me as a crazy baby mama?
Oh, the drama, the pain, the trauma.
I wanted to assault him, oh so bad,
For the betrayal that made me so mad,
But I promised my revenge, my sweet lick,
I'll show him since I'm no longer his pick.

The Nerve of The Narcissist

Oh, the dance we did, tiptoeing around,
In a world of hurt and bewilderment we found,
No marriage, no apology, just betrayal in the air,
But fear not, my friend, for humor we shall share!
I yelled out randomly, in a fit of revenge,
"I may end up in your father's bed, my friend!"
Oh, the audacity, the nerve of it all,
But little did he know I'd rise and stand tall.
Living my life for me, seeking happiness anew,
For my heart grew impatient, and hurt it did brew,
A double date my friend and I planned, a flesh call to keep it real,
But little did we know, fate had a different deal.
The Cop was supposed to be at work, but instead he sought me out,
Oh, how narcissists, always trying to keep us in doubt,
But as a victim, I started to feel myself rise,
And eventually, I did the opposite, to his surprise.
During the visit, a knock on the door,

The famous police knock, what could it be for?
I got my lick back, oh, the satisfaction I felt,
But he cursed and called me names, like a child who had
dealt.
And then, silence fell, a look of horror on my friend's face,
She asked, "Did you hear him? He used that forbidden N-
word, disgrace!"
Oh, the shock, the disbelief, my plans now changed,
But fear not, dear reader, for humor shall always remain.

Another One Bites the Dust

Oh, the funny thing that came to be,
Once I broke away, another woman quickly moved in,
you see.
A backup already in place, oh what a sight,
But I had a plan, my heart grew cold as ice.
Little did I know, I hadn't healed from the first,
Now I've encountered two narcissists, the worst.
First the grandiose, then the covert they came,
Oh, what a roller coaster, what a crazy game.
You see, when you haven't truly lived,
Breakups can leave you feeling adrift.
But fear not, for healing is on its way,
Will I heal completely? That's the question of the day.

CHAPTER THREE

Colombian Clout
Covert Narcissist

Let's call him the Colombian, a man of mystery,
Married, yet seeking thrills on a social phone line spree.
His looks could stop traffic, oh what a sight,
But little did we know, he hid his true life.
In law enforcement he served, not as my previous a simple
beat cop,
A man of value, in the shallow sense, we couldn't stop.
But oh, the drama that unfolded, unbeknownst to us all,
A covert narcissist, once more ready to make me fall.

The Physical Dummy

Oh, the dumbest decision I ever made,
After two failed relationships, I must have been swayed.
Why, oh why, did I choose a married man?
Thinking we could keep it physical, with no emotional plan.
He claimed to be honest about his situation,
But was he really, or just another fabrication?
Enamored and proud, I called him mine,
Little did I know, it was all just a funny line.

BLINDSIDED

In the realm of love, I convinced myself,
That he would leave his wife, for me, himself.
We never spoke of her, for I knew my place,
In this covert affair, a dangerous chase.
Oh, the tacky move he made one day,
Taking me along to buy an anniversary display.
I fell for him hard, blinded by desire,
Unaware of the double life he would acquire.
His job allowed him freedom, time away,
Living a secret life, day by day.
He painted a picture of unhappiness,
And I believed I could fill the void, I confess.
What made me special? I couldn't see,
My selfish desires clouded reality.
We went on a vacation, a weekend of pleasure,
But beneath the surface, a dark perversion would measure.
Red flags waved, but I turned a blind eye,
For his pleasant appearance made me sigh.

Oh, the foolishness of my infatuation,
With the Colombian, a hilarious creation.

No Lessons Applied

Oh, the tests he put me through, this Colombian man,
Questioning my every move, like he had a master plan.
My best friend warned me, said he wasn't good for me,
But I was blinded by lust, couldn't set myself free.
One fateful night, a male friend stayed over, innocent and
true.
But the Colombian saw him, and his anger just grew.
He grabbed me by the neck, spewing vile words so mean,
I was shocked and hurt, like a crushed paper scene.
I vowed to shun him, to keep him out of my life,
But he returned, apologized, and caused more strife.
Oh, the roller coaster of emotions, the ups and downs,
With this Colombian, I was seemingly bound.

THE WAKE-UP CALL

Oh, the heavenly intervention that saw,
The good and stupid in me, oh what a flaw.
He announced his departure, a blow so hard,
Desperation set in, pleading to be his card.
I tried to get a job, to relocate for him,
But my best friend's words pierced, oh so grim.
"You're being used," she said, "he doesn't want you."
Those words hit me hard, but they were true.
I cried many days, but now I see,
I was just one of many, not his only key.
Friends with benefits, at most we were,
But reopening this wound, I won't endure.
An ex is an ex, for a reason they say,
I've kept my heart guarded and moved on my way.

CHAPTER FOUR

MACHO MESS
A GRANDIOSE NARCISSIST

Now, at the marvelous age of 52,
I find myself reflecting on the choices I've made.
For 18 years, I've been with a man,
Of average intelligence, rooted in Mexico's land.
When we met, he had only three shirts,
And four pairs of pants, his English broken.
But there was something about him, I couldn't resist,
I saw potential, a project to assist.
But oh, the loving and empathetic heart in me, it seems,
Leads me astray, in matters of the heart.
For my children, who were teens at the time,
Deserved my attention, as a single mom in her prime.
Yet, here I am, with a younger spouse,
Though he doesn't look it, I must espouse.
The lessons I've learned, from all the previous deceit,
should have taught me to be wiser, in whom I meet.
So let this be a hilarious revelation,
That sometimes, our choices lead to frustration.

No plans or papers, or were there?

With this new clown, I was always bound.
Oh, the rumors I heard about his fate,
No papers, no plans, just a laborer's state.
But love bombing came, innocent and sweet,
Like a puppy at the pound, he was a treat.
Around month 3 or 4, he moved right in,
His crowded apartment, a chaotic din.
I couldn't stand it, so I took the lead,
To show him a life without such a need.
Through struggles and hardships, we pushed on,
Two beautiful children, our love had spawned.
I adopted his ways, with no plans in sight,
Hoping the struggle would lead to a bright light.

Turning a Blind Eye

Oh, the love bombing soon grew cold, it's true,
Stranded with groceries, what was I to do?
Seven months pregnant, my car wouldn't start,
I called him for help, but he didn't play his part.
No doctor's visits, no presence at either birth,
My second child premature, a struggle and worth,
But still, I stayed by his side, oh so blind,
Hoping for a future, a payoff to find.
Excuses I made, for his absence and flaws,
He was less fortunate, I'd set the right cause,
But oh, what a mess I was in with this macho man,
I held on tight, now with a hopeful plan.

HIS JOURNEY OF HIM

Oh, the years of highs and lows we faced,
But finally, our time to shine embraced.
I set everything in motion, you see,
Once he learned roofing, oh so skillfully.
With an ungrateful company, he toiled,
But our own business, I put into motion, and we finally
coiled.
Success came knocking, more and more,
But his ego grew, a bragging bore.
He envied my help, never gave me the credit due,
Claiming he did it all, oh how untrue!
In his hidden conversations, he considered me the lowly
Black woman,
Forgetting he had nothing when we began.
All I did for him, a distant memory,
But hey, I'll laugh it off, it's history!
In this macho mess, I found my way,
With patience and strength, I felt eventually I would seize
my day.

Adios

Oh, the fight or flight sensation that became my norm,
As my eyes opened wide to the truth,
The past's hurt and pain rushed in like a storm,
Leaving me bleeding, wounded, and uncouth.
So many affairs, so irresponsible,
Cutting deep, bleeding for years to come,
I don't trust anyone, it's undeniable,
Realizing I'm the common denominator, oh, what a
conundrum!
Wearing "Use me" and "I care" like a fur coat,
Empathy, a curse that binds me tight,
But I chose to walk away, to stay afloat,
Dealing with hoovering and disrespect, what a sight!
He thought he could break me, make me a shell,
But I stood strong, refusing to be his prey,
Narcissists are sad individuals, I can tell.
In my prayers, they'll stay far away.
No more patience for their toxic ways,

For this last one, who drained my youth,
He can kick rocks, and face his own maze,
I'll move forward, embracing my own truth.

THOUGHTS OF THE AUTHOR

I think if I had not read or watched the many videos regarding narcissism, I may have been wearing an orange jumpsuit today. There needs to be more awareness because people are quick to comment, the word *NARCISSIST(ic)* is so frequently used incorrectly. People who have survived narcissistic abuse and have been educated on the subject are not using the word loosely, even if their partner has not officially been diagnosed. The victim knows.

I expressed my life through poetry because it was easier to do so. I am ADHD, and I wasn't going to tell myself ANOTHER year that I was going to write a book and didn't. My last relationship was 18, almost 19 years, and he was/is a serial cheater and a liar. I have learned many more unflattering things about him since my departure in August of 2023.

This hurt is a hurt that no one should experience, but it happens when people do not give themselves time to recover from prior traumatic relationships because you are taking that baggage from place to place, and narcissists love it and will remind you of it when all is said and done. Vetting is also important, and it does not just stop at the potential significant other; it must be his or her family too. Finding out family dynamics is very important.

Grandiose narcissists are not hard to spot if you are paying attention; they go by the narcissist playbook. A covert narcissist is a little bit more difficult to detect because they give off a genuine care pretense. My advice is to take the time to get to know a person; this is key. We are not as lonely as we think we are. But neither of these types of narcissists has any hope of being a decent person if they don't open themselves up to counseling AND spirituality.

I am now in my 50s, and it seems like half of my life has been spent with narcissistic people, and yes, I will bear some of the burden because I did see flags. There are always flags, and some people will ignore the flags. I have robbed myself of true happiness for a long time but there is still hope. I will say I have gotten my so-called "lick" back a couple of times, and it felt good at the time, but no lasting fulfillment.

I wish that it was a crime to be a narcissist or just let me collect SSI for the health problems that I have either suffered or had pre-existing conditions that have worsened. It is so unfair to see them as they seemingly walk off into the sunset to screw up other lives, even though it is a cycle with them until they die. Retreating from this love thing is what is necessary for now. The only clown I want to see is Ronald McDonald.

I also want to mention that mental health is very important. I wish I could have forced my last husband to go to counseling; he has a lot of unresolved traumas. Now I must love myself and forgive myself for MANY bad decisions.

Forgiveness is key because being bitter is not an option. I have done my share of wrong things, and I want to be forgiven.

Here is a recent letter I wrote to my abuser:

I wanted to take a moment to express my thoughts and feelings, as I believe it is important for both of us to have a clear understanding of where we stand.

First and foremost, I want to acknowledge that I have forgiven you for the past. Holding onto grudges and resentment only weighs us down, and I have chosen to let go of any negative emotions that may have lingered. This forgiveness is not a sign of weakness or an indication that I condone any hurtful actions, but rather a way for me to find peace within myself.

I am grateful for the two wonderful children that we share. They are a constant reminder of the love we once had and the beautiful moments we experienced together. While our marriage may not have lasted as long as we had hoped, I understand that love can be a complex journey, and people change and grow in different directions.

I want to encourage you to prioritize your physical well-being. Taking care of oneself is essential for a fulfilling and healthy life. It is my sincere wish that you find the strength and motivation to make positive changes in this aspect of your life.

Furthermore, I urge you to stay true to yourself. We all carry our own traumas and struggles, and it is crucial to confront and make peace with them. Healing and personal growth are lifelong processes, and I genuinely hope that you find the strength and support to navigate your own journey.

As we both grow older, it becomes increasingly important to cherish the time we have and make the most of it. I have come to value this period of self-discovery, where I am getting to know myself better and building a strong foundation for my children's future. It is a time of reflection, growth, and embracing new opportunities.

While I acknowledge that there may be prospects for me in the future, I am also aware of the importance of patience. Rushing into new relationships or endeavors can often lead to disappointment and being unfulfilled. I am taking the time to focus on myself and my children, knowing that love will come when the time is right.

In closing, I want to sincerely wish you all the happiness in the world. We may have taken different paths, but I genuinely hope that you find joy, fulfillment, and peace in your life. May you embrace the opportunities that come your way and continue to grow as an individual.

With Love

I wrote this book intending to help people identify red flags and take precautions when encountering toxic or narcissistic individuals. While I cannot dictate who someone should love, it is important to prioritize one's mental and physical well-being. Consider this book as a guide to recognizing when you may become a target of such individuals. It is crucial to practice self-love healthily and **MOST IMPORTANTLY** seek a relationship with your creator, as it can assist you in making better choices and forming healthier relationships.

Please Note: My opinions are my own, I am not a licensed therapist or psychiatrist. I can only speak from my heart and my personal experiences.